**BLAST OFF!**

# ALL ABOUT
# ROCKETS

*Miriam Gross*

**PowerKiDS**
press™

New York

For Martin

Published in 2009 by The Rosen Publishing Group, Inc.
29 East 21st Street, New York, NY 10010

First Edition

Editor: Joanne Randolph
Book Design: Greg Tucker
Photo Research: Jessica Gerweck

Photo Credits: Cover, pp. 11, 13, 15, 17, 21 © Getty Images; pp. 5, 9 Shutterstock.com; p. 7 © NASA/Getty Images; p. 19 © Time & Life Pictures/Getty Images.

Library of Congress Cataloging-in-Publication Data

Gross, Miriam.
  All about rockets / Miriam Gross. — 1st ed.
      p. cm. — (Blast off!)
  Includes index.
  ISBN 978-1-4358-2735-6 (library binding) — ISBN 978-1-4358-3133-9 (pbk.)
ISBN 978-1-4358-3139-1 (6-pack)
  1. Rocketry—Juvenile literature. I. Title.
  TL793.G78 2009
  629.47'5—dc22
                                        2008028349

Manufactured in the United States of America

# CONTENTS

For hundreds of years, people dreamed of traveling to outer space. How could they ever get high enough in the sky to see the Moon up close or to study other **planets**, though?

Gravity is the force that keeps our feet on Earth so that we do not float up into the air. If you want to travel to space, you need a force that is stronger than gravity to push you up.

A rocket produces a force that is strong enough. In fact, it is the only kind of machine that is powerful enough to blast off from Earth into space.

The Pinwheel Galaxy is 27,000 light years away. Ever since rockets helped launch the Hubble Space Telescope in 1990, we can take a closer look at galaxies like this one.

A rocket works by pushing hot gas out through a hole at one end. The hole is small and the gas is pushed out very fast. This produces a force called thrust.

Pretend that you have a balloon filled with air. Then you poke a small hole in the balloon. The balloon will whiz around in the air until there is no more air left inside. This is because the air is producing thrust as it leaves the balloon through the small hole. The thrust pushes against the balloon and makes it move. Rockets work in much the same way.

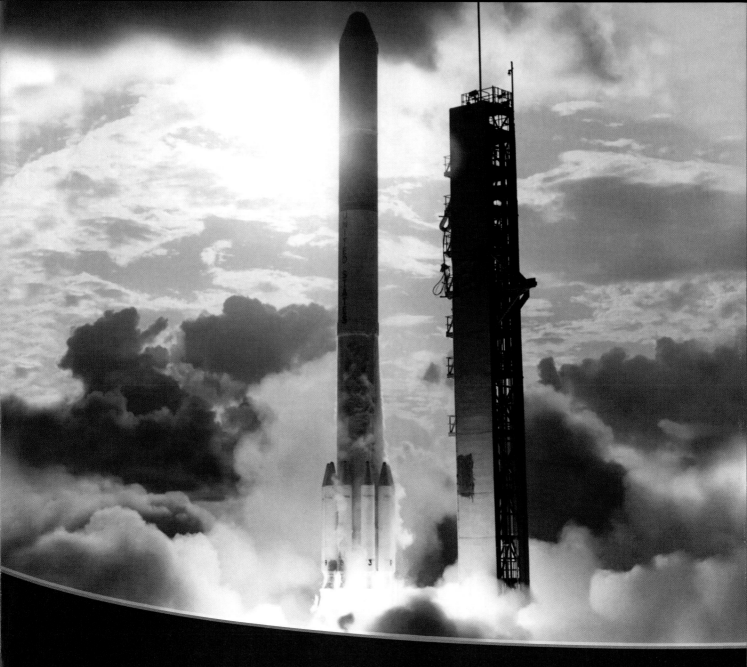

Here a rocket blasts off. All the fire and smoke shown here is the gas leaving the rocket and pushing the rocket off the ground with a huge amount of force.

A rocket has four main parts. These are the payload, the propellants, the chamber, and the nozzle. The payload sits at the top of the rocket. It is the object that the rocket carries up into space, such as a spacecraft with an **astronaut** inside. The propellant is the **fuel** that powers the rocket. The propellant burns in the chamber. The nozzle allows the propellant to leave the chamber as gas.

Some rockets are made of parts called stages. When the fuel in one stage burns up, the stage falls off. This makes the rocket lighter, so it can fly higher.

This is a close-up look at the chamber and the nozzles of the rocket. As hot gas pushes its way out through the nozzle, the force moves the rocket upward.

Rockets have many uses on Earth and in the air. Small rockets send fireworks up into the sky. They can send **signals** for help from ships in trouble. Other rockets send **bombs** to **targets** that are far away. Powerful rockets can also help some planes fly faster than the **speed of sound**. Sound travels at 760 miles per hour (1,223 km/h). That is fast!

Rockets can send tools high in the sky to study Earth's weather. They can fly people into space. They can also send up tools that let people study outer space from Earth.

NASA's X-43A plane used a Pegasus booster rocket to help it break the world speed record. It flew at Mach 7, which is seven times faster than the speed of sound.

Rockets were likely invented in China around AD 1200. Early rockets were powered by gunpowder. They were mostly used in wars, sending fire or bombs to the enemy.

An American scientist named Robert Goddard **launched** the first modern rocket in March 1926. It went up only 184 feet (56 m), but Goddard believed that rockets could go to space one day.

During **World War II**, Germany bombed England using fast, powerful V2 rockets. After the war, the United States and the **Soviet Union** studied the V2 rockets to see how they could be used to **explore** space.

Dr. Robert Goddard (left) is shown here working with other men on a rocket with the outer part removed. His ideas on rockets served as the basis for the rockets made today.

On April 12, 1961, in the Soviet Union, Yuri Gagarin launched into space aboard the *Vostok 1*. He was the first person ever to fly into space. An R-7 rocket carried *Vostok 1*'s ball-shaped capsule, the area where the astronaut sits.

*Vostok 1* rose high into the sky, flying nearly 18,000 miles per hour (28,968 km/h). Gagarin saw the sky turn from the light blue of Earth's **atmosphere** to the blackness of space. He flew up so high that he was able to orbit Earth, or fly around it in a circle. He flew all around Earth in 108 minutes.

Here Yuri Gagarin is shown getting ready for his flight on *Vostok 1*. The same kind of rocket used to launch *Vostok 1* launched Soviet spacecraft for over 50 years.

The first American in space was Alan Shepard. On May 5, 1961, he flew up in a capsule called *Freedom 7*. A Redstone rocket carried the capsule. The Redstone roared into space at 5,100 miles per hour (8,207 km/h). Shepard went up 116.5 miles (187.5 km) above Earth. After 15 minutes, he floated down to the sea in his capsule.

Shepard did not circle Earth like Gagarin. The Redstone rocket was not strong enough, so Shepard only flew up and came back down. In 1962, a larger Atlas rocket brought astronaut John Glenn into orbit in a capsule called the *Friendship 7*.

Here Alan Shepard is shown on the boat that picked him up after he splashed down in the Atlantic Ocean. The *Freedom 7* is behind him.

Putting a man into space was just the first step. Americans wanted to be the first to send a man to the Moon. In the 1960s, they created the Saturn V rocket. The Saturn V was the most powerful rocket ever sent into space.

The Saturn rocket had to be powerful. After all, it was going all the way to the Moon! In December 1968, the rocket brought the first astronauts into orbit around the Moon. In July 1969, it flew the *Apollo 11* astronauts to land on the Moon. Saturn V rockets flew to the Moon nine times.

The Saturn V stood 363 feet (110 m) high and had three stages and 11 engines. Here it is shown blasting off, carrying an Apollo spacecraft and three astronauts.

The space shuttle orbiter is a rocket ship that has wings like an airplane. It takes off like a regular rocket, with a loud roar and clouds of burning smoke. When it lands, its wings help it coast gently down to Earth. It can land on a runway like an airplane.

Earlier rockets could be used only one time. They became damaged during their flights into space. The space shuttle can fly into space and return many times.

The first space shuttle was called *Columbia*. It flew into orbit on April 12, 1981. Today, most astronauts fly into space aboard space shuttles.

The space shuttle *Discovery* is shown blasting off here. The three large parts fixed to the shuttle all drop away before the orbiter reaches space.

Some day, scientists hope to travel even farther out into space. They want to send astronauts to explore Mars or even Jupiter. They want to send tools to study faraway stars.

In order to carry people to other planets, rockets of the future must travel even faster than they do today. Rockets that travel to other planets will need to burn fuel more slowly. This way, the fuel lasts longer and the rockets can travel farther. The rockets will also have to weigh less.

Scientists hope to make rockets that are safer and less costly. This way, they can send more people into space. Maybe one day, you can fly on a rocket to Mars!

# GLOSSARY

**ASTRONAUT** (AS-troh-not)  A person who is trained to travel in outer space.

**ATMOSPHERE** (AT-muh-sfeer)  The layer, or blanket, of gases around an object in space. On Earth, this layer is air.

**BOMBS** (BOMZ)  Weapons that explode.

**EXPLORE** (ek-SPLOR)  To travel to little-known places.

**FUEL** (FYOOL)  Something used to make energy, warmth, or power.

**LAUNCHED** (LONCHT)  Pushed out or put into the air.

**PLANETS** (PLA-nets)  Large objects, such as Earth, that move around the Sun.

**SIGNALS** (SIG-nulz)  Messages, movements, or sounds that are sent to be read by others.

**SOVIET UNION** (SOH-vee-et YOON-yun)  A former country that reached from eastern Europe across Asia to the Pacific Ocean.

**SPEED OF SOUND** (SPEED UV SOWND)  The speed at which sound travels, which is 760 miles per hour (1,223 km/h).

**TARGETS** (TAR-gits)  Things that are aimed at.

**WORLD WAR II** (WURLD WOR TOO)  A war fought by the United States, Great Britain, France, and the Soviet Union against Germany, Japan, and Italy from 1939 to 1945.

# INDEX

WEB SITES

Due to the changing nature of Internet links, PowerKids Press has developed an online list of Web sites related to the subject of this book. This site is updated regularly. Please use this link to access the list:
www.powerkidslinks.com/blastoff/rockets/